OPENING CREDITS

I would like to offer thanks to the following people who have supported this book: -

Graham Huband of The Courier

Andrew Welsh – Craigie Column, The Courier

Gordon Barr of scottishcinemas.org

Richard (Fotofling Scotland)

I would especially like to extend my immense gratitude to the following person who went above and beyond to supply me with information, advice and was unfailingly kind, cheerful, supportive and patient.

David Powell, Archivist D C Thomson & Co Ltd

Thank you as well to the wonderful people of Dundee who trusted me with their memories…. some of the stories made me laugh while others were so interesting and gave a real insight into the city's social history.

This book is dedicated to my girls, Frank and, of course, my Tootie folk

THE TRAILER

I first had the idea of this book several years ago but never actually got round to doing it until now (2023). The main reason I decided to get off my butt and complete this book was because I realised that as the generations aged the memories of the Dundee cinemas would be lost. The demolition of the Odeon at the Stack and the Regal in Broughty Ferry made me more determined to get as many memories down on paper as I could. These were cinemas that I frequented and to see them turned to dust was very sad.

Dundee was the cinema capital of the UK and had more cinemas per head of population than anywhere else in the country. It is hard to believe that almost every neighbourhood in the city had its own cinema. We are not talking tiny wee buildings either; most of the cinemas housed at least 1000 seats.

For many Dundonians going to the cinema was an escape from their working lives. During the 20's to the 50's, most of the city's workforce were employed in the jute mills, down the shipyard or in other factories. Going to the cinema allowed those people the chance to escape from this greyness and be transported to another life (albeit briefly). Many of the cinemas actually planned their showings around the finishing times of the nearby factories in order to maximise attendance.

Youngsters used to be sent to the cinemas at the weekend to give their parents some peace. A few of the cinemas had their own clubs and some even their own songs.

The cinemas in Dundee were also pioneers of recycling. If you didn't have the cash, then you were able to gain entry by taking along some empty bottles or jam jars which the cinema would then cash in at the local scrap merchants.

From the earliest showing of moving pictures in the 1890's to the talkies in the 1920's Dundee cinemas evolved with the times and the peak of cinema going in the city was in the 1930's and 40's. A lot of this is also down to the fact that the cinema was the only place that you could get the news; this was particularly important during World War Two.

Despite adapting and modernising the cinemas could not compete with the Bingo revolution which came along in the 1960's. Many were converted to bingo halls while others just closed their doors.

Sadly, with the passing of time many of the Dundee cinemas were demolished. It is very sad as some of the buildings were truly architecturally beautiful. We lament the loss of these buildings but, being realistic, there was not really alternative uses for such large neighbourhood structures.

I am not sure if it is a Dundee thing but no one in Dundee actually went to the cinema; we all called them the pictures. In my youth the ones I went to were the Regal, Victoria, ABC, Odeons in the Cowgate and the Stack and the Steps. I must be a Jonah as none of them are still operating.

I have been genuinely amazed by the response I have had from local people about their memories of going to the cinema in Dundee. People have shared their own stories and I hope that this book will allow those memories to be shared, and also passed down to younger generations.

So, grab yourself a comfy seat and a cuppy and settle down for a wee read and a trip down memory lane.

C'mon Dundee folk…. Let's Go to the Pictures.

THE NEWS REEL

ABC (see also Capitol)) 7 Seagate Dundee

Having wanted to open a cinema in the city for a long time, Associated British Cinemas (ABC) finally got their wish when they purchased the Capitol from J B Milne in 1958. ABC did own the Plaza but wanted something more modern and central (they actually sold the Plaza to J B Milne).

Photo courtesy of D C Thomson & Co Ltd

ABC did a huge refurbishment of the former Capitol and unveiled the new look, now ABC cinema in 1959 with a showing of "South Pacific".

The original one screen in the ABC was huge and showed some real blockbusters such as "Ben Hur"; trust me it is so much better in 70mm film on the big screen than it could ever be in your living room over Easter!

Due to dwindling audiences, it was decided to split the ABC into two screens, and this took place in 1979. Although it meant that two films could now be shown it really took away from the whole cinema experience….it also wasn't helped that the sound proofing was not great so if you were watching a quiet film all you could hear was sound effects from the other screen coming through the wall.

The ABC was renamed the Cannon, but reverted back to the ABC before it closed its doors in 1998. Its interior was entirely stripped out and it is now a bar/club.

ALL SUPER CINERAMA (see BB Cinerama Cinema)

ALHAMBRA (also known as The State, The Whitehall Theatre) 12 Bellfield Street

The Alhambra Theatre, as it started life, was a 1150-seater building which was established by John Young in the mid-1890s. It was a very popular theatre putting on many live shows. John Young also had another theatre in Dundee called The Tivoli which was in Brown Street. Sadly, that Tivoli (which also showed films) was burned to the ground in 1924 and a new Tivoli Cinema was opened up, by Young, In Bonnybank Road.

In the early 20's former fairground entrepreneur Arthur Henderson arrived on the scene and commissioned famous local architect Frank Thomson to redesign the Alhambra to become a cinema and live show venue. Henderson sold the Alhambra in 1940 and it became a full-time cinema and was renamed The State.

J B Milne then bought the cinema in 1959 and it ran successfully under his stewardship until July 1965 when it bowed out of cinema use with a two week long run of Greta Garbo films. Milne then ran it as one of his All Square Bingo Clubs before selling it to the local Council in 1968.

In 1969 it was opened as the Whitehall Theatre which is still going strong.

ASTORIA (see B & B Picture House)

BB CINERAMA CINEMA (formerly Tay Street Cinema) 57 Tay Street

The 700-seater Cinerama actually started its life off as St Johns Church and was converted for cinema use in 1918 when a balcony was added, and it opened as the Tay Street Cinema. In 1919 it was under the ownership of George Bennell who changed the name to the B B Cinerama Cinema (a bit of a mouthful), No one is exactly sure what BB stood for – in some cases it was Britain's Best and in others Bright and Beautiful. However, the BB part of the name was dropped when it was taken over by John Pennycook in 1922. In 1930 the British Talking Pictures sound system was installed.

As was the case with so many local cinemas, it came under the ownership of J B Milne in 1962 and became the All Super Cinerama. It closed later that year and was demolished two years later in 1964.

B & B PICTURE HOUSE, (Also known as The Oxford and the Astoria) 60 Logie Street

Built in 1911 and opening in 1912 the B&B People's Picture House was short lived as it became the Oxford Picture House just 2 years later in 1914.

Taken over by A E Binnall in 1928 it was refurbished and rebranded as the Astoria and had a grand opening whereby it showed Charles Murray in "Vamping Venus" and Milton Sills in "The Hawks Nest".

Equipped with the latest BA sound system (British Acoustics) the Astoria had a stage and 3 dressing rooms, there was also seating for 900.

In 1936 it was bought by Charles Gray, and in the mid 50's the J B Milne chain took it over.

The Astoria suffered a bit of a sad fate as in 1977 it was compulsory purchased, and demolished, by Dundee Council to make way for a road improvement which sadly never happened.

BRIT CINEMA (see Regal Dundee)

BRITANNIA PICTURE HOUSE (see Regal Dundee)

BROADWAY (Formerly the Picture House) (Formerly the Empress Playhouse) 7 Arthurstone Terrace

Built on the corner of Arthurstone Terrace and Erskine Street, this cinema originally opened its doors as the Picture House in 1914. Built with a tin roof and with rows of wooden seats, the Picture House was renamed the Empire Playhouse in 1928.

In 1932 it was sold to Shands and underwent major redesign by architects Allan & Firskin and was renamed the Broadway. It was a mix of a cinema and live theatre and was used by Dundee Operatic for many productions. At its peak it could seat 1,023 people.

Further alterations took place in 1939 and a year later it was taken over by local cinema magnate J B Milne and was adapted for Cinemascope.

In 1963 it suffered the same fate as many cinemas, being taken over for use as a Bingo Hall (all Square Bingo Club). The building was demolished around 1991.

CAIRD HALL City Square

The 2300 seater Caird Hall was built between 1914 and 1923 as a concert hall and was opened by the then Prince of Wales on 26 October 1923. The reason work took so long was due to the outbreak of World War One. Probably most famous for its 50 pipe Harrison & Harrison organ, the Caird Hall also has a built in Bioscope projector which allows it to be used to show films.

One of the early silent movies, "Diorama" by William Hamilton was screened in the Caird Hall in 1920; it wasn't until the 1930's 'though that films began to be shown on a fairly regular basis. In

1938 a new sound system was installed in the Hall. John Pennycook showed films, including news reels, during World War Two.

The Caird Hall is a class A listed building and is now mainly used for concerts and shows.

CAPITOL (formerly Her Majesty's Theatre & Opera House) (formerly Majestic Theatre) (formerly Her Majesty's Theatre)   7 Seagate

This was originally opened in 1885 as Her Majesty's Theatre and Opera House and put on live performances of opera, drama and comedy plays. In 1915 it started screening films and, four years later was a full time cinema.

In 1925 the name was changed to Her Majesty's Picture Theatre, and it closed as this in October 1929 for redevelopment.

Just over a year later, In December 1930 it reopened as the Majestic Theatre by the J B Milne Theatre chain and was very popular. Sadly, on 28 August 1941 the cinema was destroyed by fire and subsequently demolished.

Eventually in the 1950's the cinema was rebuilt and rebranded as the Capitol, opening on 6 August 1956.

There would be a later rebranding and redevelopment of this cinema in later years when it became the ABC (see separate listing)

CINEWORLD (formerly UGC) Camperdown Leisure Park, Kingsway West

Opened under the UGC name in September 1999 this 9-screen multiplex has 1830 seats with the individual cinema screens range in seating capacity from 79 to 512.

It was rebranded as Cineworld in July 2005. As of October 2023, it is still operational.

DUNDEE CONTEMPORARY ARTS (DCA) 152 Nethergate

The 2 cinemas at DCA are part of the whole Arts building which was designed by leading architects Richard Murphy Associates of Edinburgh. Although it has digital projection (and since 2011 3D capacity) the cinemas can still show 35mm films which allows them to screen classic older films. DCA has 294 seats and was opened in March 1999 and, as of October 2023, is still in operation.

EDWARDS PICTURE PALACE – see Tivoli

ELECTRIC THEATRE William Street,

Believed to be the first actual moving picture house in Dundee. This was basically just a pop up event – a canvas roof with wooden sides which operated from 1893 to the early 1900's. It was operated by John Pennycook and was believed to have originally been situated in William Street. It also showed some theatre and drama events.

ELECTRIC THEATRE 2 122 Nethergate,

This theatre, which also housed a tearoom, first opened in 1911 under the management of J Bannister Howard and was owned by Peter Feathers. Feathers was a pioneer of early film and showed several short films of workers leaving the mills and also trains travelling across the Tay to Fife.

There is not much information on this cinema, although it is thought that it was sold to John Pennycook around 1918 who moved from his pop up in William Street to here.

It closed in 1923 and became a jewellery shop,

EMPRESS PLAYHOUSE (see Broadway)

EMPIRE (NEW EMPIRE) 62 Rosebank Street

Compared to other cinemas, and I may be being very unfair, but the exterior of the Empire was not as attractive as many of the city cinemas.

Originally opened in 1903 as a theatre, it began to show films in 1908 and was subsequently sold as a cinema in 1910.

The Empire suffered a fire in 1914 but was rebuilt. The cinema had seating for 800 and was sold to the George Singleton company in 1927 and then again in 1937, this time to the ODEON company.

It closed in 1957 and, following a fire, was demolished in 1962. There is now housing on the site.

FOREST PARK CINEMA Forest Park Road/Place

Built in just a few months by local builders Grays, the 1150 seater Forest Park opened its doors on Hogmanay 1928 with the film "Two Little Drummers" starring the very Scottish sounding child actor Wee Georgie Wood.

Photo courtesy of D C Thomson & Co Ltd

Equipped with the British Acoustic sound system, the Forest Park closed in 1967.

GAIETY (see Victoria)

GAUMONT (see Kings)

Photo courtesy of D C Thomson & Co Ltd

GILFILLAN HALL 22 Whitehall Crescent

Similar to the YMCA in Constitution Road, the Gilfillan was granted a Cinematograph Licence in 1910, although it had been showing moving pictures since January 1897.

The Gilfillan regularly showed films from February 1910 until the end of World Ward One.

GREENS PLAYHOUSE 106 Nethergate.

This is probably the most famous former cinema in Dundee. It had a massive 4132 seats and was just beautiful. If you copy this link, you will see the promotional film made for the opening of Greens.

Scotlandonscreen.org.uk/browse-films/007-000-002-095-C

With a Chromolux lighting system and the Latest Western Electrics sound system plus air conditioning and heating Greens was opened with the slogan "Its Good, Its Greens".

Opened and operated by George Green cinemas (who had 24 other cinemas), it was the most majestic in the entire chain. Designed by architect John Fairweather, assisted by Joseph Emberton many know the 83 ft tower at the entrance which stood, like a beacon for those in Dundee.

Greens seating allowed for 2576 in the stalls with 1456 in the circle. There were also 10 boxes that could seat a further 100. The way the building was designed it meant that the stalls were actually below street level. The cinema also housed the "golden divans" or "dive-ins" as they were known locally. These were areas where one could recline with a special person and hide behind curtains….there is many a story to be told there!

To ensure maximum viewing pleasure there were no pillars in the Greens with the balcony supported by a 30 tonne girder which ran the whole width of the building.

The inside certainly sounds glorious as reported by The Evening Telegraph newspaper who commented, after visiting the premises for the opening, *"First impressions on viewing the interior of the Playhouse are of amazement that such a compact building should contain the tremendous number of 4,100 seats. Immediately the question arises, "How did they get them in?"*

"Going on the analogy of the old saying that you can't get a quart into a pint pot, one would imagine that for such accommodation a building of tremendous vastness was necessary. Yet the Playhouse interior is far from overpowering in its vastness.

"There are no faraway recesses about the Playhouse.

"At the back of the balcony or the stalls one is still at reasonable distance from the screen, and the banks of seats are so arranged that there is an uninterrupted view for every part of the house.

"Another feature of the Playhouse is its decoration. The plaster is finished mainly in deep and light golds, which reflect the play of the concealed lighting in all its lovely colours."

Greens also had a very popular café, complete with specially designed crockery which was white with green rings and the name of the cinema on them.

Greens opened its doors on 3 March 1936 with a double bill featuring silver screen stars Joan Blondell and Alice Brady who were both very popular actresses of the time.

A lot of screen stars visited Greens over the years including Bob Hope, Clayton Moore (the Lone Ranger), Charles Laughton and Anna Neagle.

In the mid 60's the lovely Greens was sold to the Mecca organisation and, very sadly, was converted for bingo. It is still used for bingo.

One of the saddest days for Dundonians was 26 August 1995 when Greens/Mecca suffered a massive fire. This did see the listed building status of Greens changed from category A to Category B (and even that was just for the tower). The Tower was rebuilt.

When you ask Dundonians about this building most will still call it "Greens". The tower is still one of the most prominent landmarks in Dundee.

Photo courtesy of Richard aka Fotofling Scotland

END OF A GOLDEN ERA

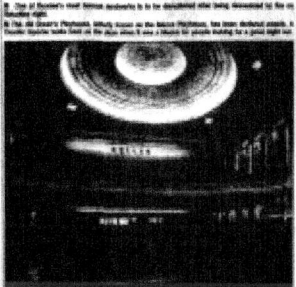

THE COURIER

KICKED INTO A NEW AGE

ON SHOW

A TEMPLE FALLS

Whatever happened to Mount Godwin-Austen?

Craigie

Council should put people before profit

WEATHERBOARD

GRAYS (Formerly Shands, formerly West End) 5 Shephards Loan

On 28 November 1912 the 772 seater West End Cinema opened its doors. Five years later it was taken over by D Shand and renamed the Shand's Picture House. In 1934 it was taken over my C R W Gray and, as seemed to be the custom, was renamed after him as Gray's Picture House.

As you can see the roof was iron and this resulted in it being an incredibly noisy affair for patrons when it rained heavily or, more often, when wee laddies would throw stones onto the roof for fun.

Photo courtesy of D C Thomson & Co Ltd

Grays had 900 seats and used the Film Industries sound system. In 1944 it had its final name change – to Gray's Cinema. It closed in 1958 and was subsequently demolished.

HER MAJESTY'S PICTURE THEATRE see Capitol

HER MAJESTY'S THEATRE & OPERA HOUSE (see Capitol)

HIPPODROME (see Princess)

KINNAIRD (formerly The Corn Exchange and Public Halls) 6 Bank Street

Photo courtesy of D C Thomson & Co Ltd

Starting life as the Corn Exchange and Public Hall, the Kinnaird was designed by architect Charles Edward and opened in 1858. In 1865 an organ was installed in the building and it became the Kinnaird Hall and was used for meetings, lectures etc. One of those who spoke there was Winston Churchill who, for 14 years was MP for Dundee (1908-1922). He was not hugely popular in the city as he only visited once a year. He did, rather foolishly, once describe the city as his "seat for life".

As legend has it (and I can't vouch for the truth of this), he arrived at the Kinnaird with the help of some local men who carried him in (apparently, he had a leg injury). He allegedly paid the men a pound to bring him in to the hall. No sooner had he arrived than the crowed helpfully offered the men two pounds if they would take him back out!

Photo courtesy of D C Thomson & Co Ltd

In the 1890s the Kinnaird was also used as a roller skating rink and in 1897 it screened its first moving picture show, converting to a full time cinema in 1919.

In 1928 the capacity of the Kinnaird was 1476 seats and RCA sound installed. The cinema was renamed the Kinnaird Picture House.

In 1944 J B Milne took over the Kinnaird and 10 years later Cinemascope was installed with this being unveiled at a screening of "The Coins in the Fountain". The Kinnaird closed its doors as a cinema in 1962 and sadly was ruined by fire on 2 January 1966.

KINGS (also known as Gaumont) (also known as ODEON) 27 Cowgate

Along with the Greens Playhouse, the Kings is the cinema that most Dundonians think about when you ask them about movie theatres in the city.

The Kings Theatre and Hippodrome opened its doors on 15 March 1909 and was designed by local architects Frank and Henry Thomson.

It was beautifully designed in the baroque style and, at its peak, could accommodate 2227 people in the stalls, dress circle, balcony and boxes. With a marble proscenium and a domed ceiling, the Kings also boasted beautifully painted frescos on the walls.

On 2 April 1909 the Kings showed its first film, and it was subsequently granted the coveted Cinematograph Licence in 1910. It was still used as a theatre and attracted such acts as Harry Lauder who appeared in 1916. In September 1928 it was bought by Provincial Theatre Cinematograph and a Wurlitzer organ was installed which meant the boxed seats were closed. The balcony was also closed, and the capacity reduced to 1458.

In 1929 the Gaumont British Theatre company bought over the Provincial Theatre group and the cinema changed its name to the Gaumont in May 1950.

Photo courtesy of D C Thomson & Co Ltd

During the Second World War the King`s shut for the duration as a cinema but became the Garrison Theatre. From 1941 to 1945 it staged over 200 variety shows, revues and concerts usually on Sundays for uniformed personnel and their guests. At the end of the war, it reverted to its normal name King`s Theatre

Photo courtesy of D C Thomson & Co Ltd

In 1961 (in what I would call an appalling act), the interior of this building was remodelled, and a suspended ceiling put in covering the dome and the proscenium. In 1973, following the closure of the ODEON (Vogue) in Strathmartine Road, it was renamed the ODEON and became solely a cinema.

The ODEON used to show a double bill of films on a loop which meant you could go in half way through the first film and watch it until the end, then watch the second film and, if you were so inclined, stay in your seat to watch the first half of the film you missed.

In October 1981 the cinema closed and two years later became a bingo hall. In more recent years it has been a nightclub and bar. Apparently the remains of the beautiful original interior can be found boarded in behind the newer works; I can't say for sure that this is true, but it would be nice to think it was.

As a side note the owners of the Kings Theatre also owned the building next door which had its own separate entrance from the street which took patrons to the Kings bar "The Bodega". This was very popular and in subsequent years became the Continental Ballroom and Restaurant.

LA SCALA 30 Murraygate

The 1099 seater La Scala was most famous for its 18 piece Orchestra which was conducted by Routledge Bell. So impressive was this orchestra that they were asked to perform in their own right, away from the cinema. This was probably the reason why (the) La Scala was the last cinema in the city to welcome the talkies, not installing a sound system until 1931 – a good two years behind other local picture houses.

Photo courtesy of D C Thomson & Co Ltd

People often forget that while the "talkies" were a real revolution in terms of the cinematic experience, it sadly meant that many hundreds of talented musicians lost their jobs.

In fairness to (the) La Scala although they were behind the times when it came to the "talkies", it was actually the first purpose built cinema in Dundee to be built solely for the moving picture.

It closed in 1965 to make way for the then Woolworths store to expand. The wonderful dome of (the) La Scala was demolished in 1984.

MAIN STREET PICTURE PALACE (see Regent)

MAJESTIC THEATRE (see also Capitol and ABC)

Photo courtesy of D C Thomson & Co Ltd

NEW BRITANNIA (see Regal Dundee)

NEW CINEMA (see Ritz)

NEW PALLADIUM (see Rex)

NEW PICTURE HOUSE (see Broadway)

ODEON AT THE STACK Harefield Road (Stack Leisure Park)

The six screen 1,646 seater multiplex was opened on 15 June 1993 by the cast of popular TV Police drama "Taggart". Its late star Mark McManus cut the ribbon and said the works "Okay Dundee, Let's go to the Pictures".

Image courtesy of www.scottishcinemas.org

The screens had the following capacities 574, 210, 216, 233, 192 and 221.

The cinema was the first multiplex in Dundee and was very popular, although its location was probably not the best., being so far from the city centre.

I do recall 'though when "Braveheart" was shown there was near riots at coming out time with patrons all set to march South to seek vengeance! It was also here that I sat through all four hours of "Hamlet", which was kindly split into two parts to allow for viewers to grab a toilet break and some more munchies.

The Odean closed on 4 March 2001 and was replaced with another ODEON, a 10 screen cinema in the other end of Dundee. It was demolished in 2023.

ODEON COWGATE (see Kings)

Photo courtesy of D C Thomson & Co Ltd

ODEON LUXE DOUGLASFIELD Douglas Road

Build to replace the ODEON at the Stack, this cinema opened in November 2001 and had an original capacity of 2581 seats spread over 10 cinemas. The cinemas themselves ranged in seating capacity from 104 to 483.

In 2019 it underwent a rebrand to become an ODEON LUXE and was refurbished to include reclining seats. The refurb meant that the seating capacity was reduced to 881. As of October 2023, it is still operational.

ODEON (formerly the Vogue) 146 Strathmartine Road

Designed in the Art Deco Style by Glasgow architect James McKissack, this cinema originally opened on 21 September 1936 as the Vogue which was part of the George Singleton chain of picture houses. The first film to be screened was a Shirley Temple film "The Littlest Rebel."

In March 1937 the cinema was bought over by the Oscar Deutsch chain (ODEON Cinemas) who took over 10 of the Singleton cinemas. However, it took a full year before the name of the cinema actually changed.

This cinema had 1533 seats – 1011 were in the front with a further 523 on a raised section at the rear. In addition, it housed a stage and a couple of dressing rooms.

The Odeon was very popular with children as it ran a hugely successful children's club with "Uncle Bill" who was the projectionist. Those who attended the club received a special card on their birthdays.

Sadly, this cinema was closed on 24 February 1973 to be demolished and replaced by a supermarket.

Despite popular myth ODEON did not stand for Oscar Deutsch Entertains Our Nation.

OXFORD (see B & B Picture House)

PALACE (formerly Savoy) (formerly Electric) (formerly People's Palace) (formerly Theatre Royal)   160 Nethergate

Photo courtesy of D C Thomson & Co Ltd

This cinema/theatre was built on a site that used to house a circus and also the Jollity Theatre which was burned to the ground. The People's Palace had originally been at the bottom of the Lochee Road in 1891.

In 1893 the building, designed by J J Hutton, opened its doors as a theatre and began showing films in 1909 and became a full time cinema in 1912.

It was renamed the Savoy in 1910 and then was sold to SCVT and was rebranded as the Palace in 1924 with the screening of "blood and Sand" starring Rudolph Valentino.

In 1938 it closed its doors as a cinema and became the Palace Theatre. This was probably due to the opening of the Greens Playhouse just down the road. It had many successful years as a theatre. It showed many acts from across the country and for several years was run by the Alexander Brothers as the Theatre Royal.

As with many theatres/cinemas it became a victim of the bingo revolution and then was a disco for a short period of time. It suffered a fire in 1977 and was subsequently demolished.

PALLADIUM (see Rex)

PAVILLION (see Rex)

PEOPLE'S PALACE (see Palace)

PLAZA 107 Hilltown

The 1620 seater Plaza was another cinema designed by the architects McLaren, Souter and Salmond for Scottish Cinema and Variety Theatres and opened its doors in May 1928. It was taken over by the ABC chain (Associated British Cinemas) in 1929 before being bought over by the J B Milne group in 1958. It closed in 1972, however had a brief reprieve in 1975 when it became a bingo hall complete with a small cinema. This only lasted a year, and the Plaza closed its doors for the last time in 1976.

Photo courtesy of D C Thomson & Co Ltd

Like so many other cinemas its fate was to be a fire and the site was cleared to make room for housing.

PRINCESS (Formerly Hippodrome) 160 Hawkhill

The Princess started life as the Hippodrome Theatre in 1908 and then began to show films in 1912.

Photo courtesy of D C Thomson & Co Ltd

After the First World War it was renamed the Princess Theatre and housed a stage and 3 dressing rooms. It was a very grand theatre with 704 seats, and quite dramatic with the arch in front of the stage at the roof extending to some 26ft wide.

The Princess closed its doors in 1959 and has sadly since been demolished.

REGAL (DUNDEE) (formerly Brit Cinema) (formerly New Britannia) (formerly Salon) (formerly Britannia Picture House) 39 Smalls Wynd

The 1000 seater Regal, Dundee was only open for 50 years but had a ridiculous number of names! It first opened its doors in 1911 as the Britannia Picture House before being rebranded as the Salon in 1923 and then rebranded again as the Britannia just two years later.

In 1936 it was bought over by J B Milne who installed the British Thomson-Houston sound system and renamed the cinema again – this time to the New Britannia, changing its identity again to the Brit a few years later.

In 1940 it finally received its last name change to the Regal and it remained as such until 1963 when the University of Dundee bought it over and demolished it to make way for educational buildings.

REGENT (previously on site Main Street Picture Palace) 20 Main Street

In 1912 the Main Street Picture House opened its doors, however it was demolished a few years later and the Regent was built in its stead, opening in 1922.

With 1000 seats, the Regent was originally owned by the same company that had the Tivoli (Edwards and Fraser), however it was sold to Prain Brothers before sadly closing in 1961. It became a bingo hall.

REX (formerly New Palladium) (formerly Palladium) (formerly Pavilion) 67 Alexander Street

This was the first cinema to be owned by J B Milne who was to eventually own a whole string of cinemas across Scotland. It is a cinema that, I must confess, I have a soft spot for.

Built by John Pennycook (who would later own several local cinemas), the Rex opened its doors as the Pavilion in 1913 with seating for 830. When it opened the Pavilion was a very basic corrugated iron structure. As you can see the seating was on one level with no balcony. In 1920 it was renamed the Palladium and underwent another name change in 1926 when it was sold to Hymen Cohen and rebranded as the New Palladium.

Two years later J B Milne bought it over and in 158 he completely refurbished it and, I kid you not, renamed it after his dog Rex! It closed its doors in 1961 and was demolished to make way for housing.

RIALTO 1 Grays Lane Lochee

The 1168 seater Rialto suffered a bit of an identity crisis regarding its look - for while the exterior was built in the Mexican style the interior was given a Chinese look. The projection box itself was in the shape of a face with the holes for the lighting depicting eyes. The barrel vaulted roof and the walls were decorated with Chines images of snakes and dragons.

Photo courtesy of D C Thomson & Co Ltd

The Rialto opened in 1928 by John Pennycook and housed a Western Electric sound system.

The original Rialto layout also saw the orchestra playing from a "Chinese" bridge sited in the ornate Chinese garden interior. The seating was like that of a stadium with a raised section at the back and no overhanging circle.

In 1929 it became the first cinema in Dundee to show a full length talking film. The location of the Rialto was excellent and showings were timed to allow those working in the nearby Mills to finish their shifts, grab a quick fish supper and head to the cinema.

It was taken over in the mid 50's by J B Milne and ran very successfully until 1962 when Milne converted it to one of his All Square Bingo Houses. Bingo continued in the Rialto until about 1990.

Interestingly the Rialto was also the place where Scottish boxing legend Ken Buchanan held his last amateur fight; he turned professional in 1965.

In 1933 the Rialto building was given Grade B Listed status. This was supposed to protect the building from demolition, and it was always hoped that after the bingo closed another use could be found.

Sadly in 2007 the Rialto suffered a fire which despite causing smoke damage did not damage the structure of the building. The owner fought for a long time to have the listing removed to allow him to demolish the building. Eventually, due to fears for children playing in the empty building, its listed status was removed, and demolition went ahead.

The Rialto has been replaced by housing.

RITZ (formerly the New Cinema, formerly the Stobswell Cinema)
Mains Loan

Opening in 1910 by owner Peter Feathers, the New Cinema was a rather basic building design. There was no ceiling in the auditorium which meant the roof trusses were exposed to all. The building housed 850 seats. Although the building itself was basic it was Dundee's first purpose built cinema.

Photo courtesy of D C Thomson & Co Ltd

In 1914 it was renamed as the Stobswell Cinema and ran as this until 1931 when it underwent refurbishment and reverted back to its original name of New Cinema.

As seems to have been the case with many cinemas, there was a fire in in May 1945 and was closed until 1948.

The J B Milne Theatre chain took it over in 1959 and renamed it the Ritz Cinema. It seems to have been a bit of an unlucky building as it suffered 2 more fires; the first was in 1961 and another blaze occurred in September 1970.

The Ritz closed in 1973 and was demolished to make way for housing.

ROYAL PICTURE HOUSE (see Royal)

ROYAL 22 Arthurstone Terrace

Designed by McLaren, Soutar and Salmond (who also designed the Royalty a few streets away), the Royal was on the corner of Arthurstone Terrace and Erskine Street and could seat 900.

It opened around 1910 and was redeveloped a few years later. The dome was an impressive 36 feet wide. In 1931 a Western Electric (WE) sound system was installed, and the cinema rebranded as the Royal Picture House. It closed as a cinema in 1962 and then became a bingo hall, before being demolished to make way for flats in 2006.

ROYALTY KINEMA 62 Watson Street

Another cinema controlled by J B Milne, the 835 seater Royalty was opened in 1919 and was designed by architects McLaren, Soutar and Salmond. It was closed in 1965 and replaced by housing. The Royalty was sited right on the corner of Watson Street and Baffin Street.

Photo courtesy of D C Thomson & Co Ltd

SALON (see Regal Dundee)

SAVOY (see Palace)

SHAND (see Grays)

STATE (see Alhambra)

STEPS THEATRE Wellgate Centre

Opened in the late 1970's the Steps was housed in the Wellgate Centre which was a popular shopping mall with the cinema and Council run library on the top floor. It was a part time cinema which only showed films on certain days. It was also utilised as a conference centre and theatre. The Steps specialised in showing foreign language and art films and rarely showed the mainstream films that were popular at other local cinemas. The seats in the cinema were a very vivid green. For its 20th anniversary they asked local people which films they wanted to see. I worked in PR with the Council (owners of the Steps) and was tasked with promoting this……I did tell everyone I knew to submit their votes. Somehow 'though I don't think the many submissions asking for various Western films was quite the response that had been hoped for (think more French art-house) and the poll was quietly shelved which was a shame as I, and many others, would have liked to see The Magnificent Seven on the big screen. As of October 2023, the Steps is still in use as a conference centre.

STOBSWELL (see Ritz)

TAY STREET CINEMA (see B B Cinerama)

THEATRE ROYAL (see Palace))

THEATRE ROYAL Castle Street

I did not intend to include this as it was just a Theatre and never showed films – it was sited above what was Keillors China Shop. That said, Castle Street was the site of a photographic studio across the road (Above Braithwaites Coffee) and it was here that the first public performance of an actual moving film took place.

TIVOLI (TIVOLI CONTINENTAL) (formerly Edwards Picture Palace) 20 Bonnybank Road

Originally built and opened in Brown Street the original Tivoli was operated by John Young and had 1,000 seats. Also known for a period as Edwards, it was rebranded by Tivoli in 1913 before being seriously damaged by a fire in 1924.

Image courtesy of www.scottishcinemas.org

With the insurance money Young moved the cinema to Bonnybank Road where it was the Tivoli that most Dundonians remember. In the 1950's it began to show some "Continental" films – films that were rather racy for the times. This saw it renamed as the Tivoli Continental. Despite its sexy reputation, the owners of the Tivoli were a delightful couple and served patrons with sandwiches and tea in the cinemas tea room. It closed its doors on 27 August 1997 to become a snooker hall.

TIVOLI CONTINENTAL (see Tivoli)

UGC (see Cineworld)

VICTORIA (formerly Gaiety) 92 Victoria Road

The then 960 seater Royal Victoria Theatre was designed by McCulloch & Fairley and opened in the 1840's as a variety theatre. Under plans created by architect William Alexander it underwent redevelopment and upgrading in 1903 and in 1905 it changed its name to the Gaiety Theatre.

It started to show films in December 1905, and, at that time, electric lighting was installed in the building. In 1910 it fell under the brief ownership of R C Buchanan and he sold it to Victoria Cinema Ltd in 1920 when it was renamed. The Victoria is one of several Dundee cinemas that lays claim to being the first full time cinema in the city.

In the 1930s the Victoria reverted back to showing live theatre shows with just the occasional film. However British Thomson Houston (BTH) sound was installed in 1935 and the building taken over by cinema magnate J B Milne who changed it back to sole cinema use.

Although originally a pleasant place a lot of people recall that the cinema did have rather "grumpy" staff. The cinema, certainly in latter years, suffered from a chronic lack of investment and it became known locally as "the flea pit".

I can testify personally that the Victoria was in a very sad state in later years – a rat ran over my foot at one of its last showings.

Photo courtesy of D C Thomson & Co Ltd

Photo courtesy of D C Thomson & Co Ltd

The Victoria had two balconies, the top one being known locally as "the gods". It continued to show films until the building was condemned in 1989.

VOGUE (See ODEON Strathmartine Road)

WEST END (see Grays)

WELLINGTON CINEMA Wellington Street

Opened in 1906 and one of several cinemas in Dundee that lay claim to being the first actual cinema in the city. It was built by Arthur Henderson who went on to remodel the Alhambra (Whitehall Theatre).

WHITEHALL THEATRE (see Alhambra)

YMCA 10 Constitution Road

This building is often forgotten about, but it was indeed a cinema for a time, albeit on an occasional basis.

The YMCA first showed films on 15 October 1857. After a bit of a hiccup between August 1910 and September 1910 with the granting of the Cinematograph Licence, the YMCA continued to screen films until 1930, bowing out with Maureen O'Sullivan and Charles Laughton in "Sentence Deferred".

The Cinematograph Licence was revoked at that time as the building was deemed unsafe for cinema use.

BROUGHTY FERRY CINEMAS

BROUGHTY FERRY PICTURE HOUSE (see Reres)

GRAND THEATRE (see New Grand)

NEW GRAND CINEMA (Kings Street)

Originally opened as the Grand Theatre around 1911, this building had long wooden benches as seats and a corrugated iron roof, which was very noisy during rain showers.

Renamed the New Grand Cinema in 1931, it was demolished in 1940 to make way for housing.

REGAL 51 Queen Street

Opened in 1870 as a training hall for the First Forfarshire Artillery Volunteers, the Regal came into being as a cinema in 1936 under the ownership of the Arbroath Cinema Company. It had seating for 712.

Photo courtesy of D C Thomson & Co Ltd

During the conversion to a cinema, the interior was completely refurbished and many of the decorative elements came from the recently decommissioned White Star Ocean liner called the Homeric, which also provided the interior for the Rex cinema in Stonehouse. White Star, of course, being famous for the Titanic.

The Regal was very popular with local youngsters who attended the Saturday afternoon matinee. It was run by two spinster sisters, the Misses Humphries who always wore black.

In 1978 the Regal became a part time cinema with bingo being offered the rest of the time. It finally closed altogether in 1991. The Regal then became adjacent to a car showroom and despite it being a B listed building it was demolished altogether in summer 2023.

RERES (formerly Broughty Ferry Picture House) Gray Street

The 500 seater Reres was also known locally as The Ranch as it frequently showed Western films.

It originally opened in 1914 as the Broughty Ferry Picture House and was designed by prominent local architect Frank Thomson.

In 1930 it, like the Regal in the Ferry, was fell under the ownership of the Arbroath Cinema Company and its name was changed to the Reres. It closed in 1962 and is now a launderette.

THE SHORTS

* You will have noticed that many of the cinemas suffered fires. This was due to the highly flammable film material. Sadly, many cinema owners were not happy at having to pay firemen and this was brought home to roost in 1914 when the then Empire was burnt to the ground. In 1906 the Dundee Firemaster made a report to the local Council asking that all projection equipment and film material be placed in a fireproof box and that a member of the Fire Brigade be present at all film shows (as they were at theatre productions). This was implemented in July 1906 and that year 946 showings were attended by the fire service. To highlight the growth of the popularity of cinemas by 1912 6246 showings were attended.

* The 1909 Cinematograph Act made it a legal requirement to get a licence before you could show any films in a public place. The first cinemas in Dundee to obtain such a licence were Kinnaird Hall, People's palace, Empire Theatre, YMCA, Gilfillan Hall, Main Street, King's Theatre, Foresters Hall, St Mary Magdalene's Hall and Blackness Quarry Theatre.

*1962 was the worst year for Dundee cinemas when 7 closed. This was mainly due to the move from cinema to bingo. Some cinema owners such as J B Milne ran their own successful bingo companies when cinema went into decline.

*Cinema building in Dundee really took off from 1910 when numerous cinemas began to appear in neighbourhoods across the city.

*At its peak, Dundee had 25 cinemas which worked out at approx. one cinema for every 6400 people which was way higher than even Glasgow whose ratio was one per 8200.

*Moving pictures first appeared in Dundee in 1895/6

The first talking movie was The Jazz Singer which premiered on 6 October 1927. The first full length talkie was shown in Dundee at The Rialto in Lochee in 1929. In 1929, Victor Hamilton who was managing director of the Kinnaird Cinema spoke to the Dundee Rotary Club and had this to say about the future of cinemas…"I feel convinced the talkies will survive and I further believe that most pictures will be in colour."*

THE LEADING MAN

I don't think any book about cinemas in Dundee would be complete without a nod to J B Milne, a man whose name you will have seen many times.

The story of this man who went on to own 38 cinemas across Scotland is really quite remarkable and, truth be told, is probably worth a film of its own. J B Milnes story is that of a man from very humble beginnings who dared to dream big and whose dream actually did come true….

Born one of three sons to a local coal merchant, John (McLeod) Bannerman Milne was born in Dundee in 1902. He was a highly talented musician and at the age of nine he bought his first violin. When he was 16, Milne worked in Dura works from 5.30am until 6pm at night; he then taught violin lessons until 8pm when he moved on to his third job, playing in a dance hall until midnight!

Although he had a good position at Dura, his heart was in music and entertainment, and he moved to a job at the Variety Theatre (Palladium/Rex). Earning 19s a week as musical director and cleaner he saved enough money to invest in a motor hire business.

In 1928 he sold the hire business to buy the Palladium for £360 which he later renamed the Rex, after his Labrador dog.

Milne saw the move from the silent screen to talkies and ensured his cinemas were up to date. It is said that he refused to show trailers for forthcoming events as he saw this as free advertising for the film companies.

Milne also refused to stock any other confectionary in his cinemas other than Welch's; in fact, one of his cinema managers was the local company rep.

As cinema attendance declined in the 60's, Milne made the move to bingo and formed All Square Bingo which he reverted many of his cinemas to. Milne died, aged 66 in September 1968.

As a tribute to his love of music a traditional Scottish tune was created in his memory, and it is said that the first 8 bars of this tune represent the auditions for leading man and leading lady.

Some have reported that Milne was not the easiest of men to work for…. but I think that any man who named a cinema after their dog has to be pretty decent. He certainly knew his stuff when it came to the cinema business.

Cinemas owned by J B Milne were:

ABC (Dundee) , Alhambra (Dunfermline), Angus Playhouse (Montrose) Arc Cinema (Peterhead), Astoria (Edinburgh), Astoria (Dundee), Broadway (Dundee) County (Kinross), Globe (Buckhaven), Grays (Dundee), King's (Montrose), Kinnaird (Dundee), Kino (Leven), La Scala (Cupar), Majestic (Dundee), New Picture House (Cowdenbeath), New Tivoli Picture House (Edinburgh), North Star (Lerwick), Opera (Lochgelly), Palace (Methil), Palace (Arbroath), Pavilion (Galasheils), Picture House (Banff), Picture House (Tayport), Playhouse (Stornoway), Playhouse (Peterhead), Plaza (Dundee), Regal (Macduff), Regal (Blairgowrie), Regal (East Wemyss), Regal (Dundee), Regal (Auchterarder), Rex (Dundee), Rialto (Dundee), Ritz (Dundee), Ritz (Crieff), Royalty Kinema (Dundee), Troxy (Leven), Tudor (Edinburgh), Victoria (Dundee), Whitehall (Dundee)

THE LEADING LADIES

Since I have included a leading man, J B Milne in this book, I feel it is only fair of me have a leading lady as well. In this case 'though I am going for two ladies.

While these ladies may not have been cinema magnates like Milne, to me they were the face of cinema when I was growing up. These ladies are the Humphries sisters who ran the Regal in Broughty Ferry for several decades.

The Misses Humphries were ladies who both always wore black, or dark coloured dresses, with perhaps a pearl necklace or brooch. They both had short grey hair and, to me they seemed ancient. I have to say that I was five when I started going to the Regal so everyone seemed old. Looking back, I would imagine they were probably in their late 50's or 60's – which is not really old at all!

The ladies did everything in the Regal themselves, from taking your entrance fee to manning the kiosk at the interval. The choice, for your 10p was either a Kia-ora orange juice or a strawberry "Mivi" ice lolly.

These ladies were firm, but fair and put up with no nonsense from the squads of us who attended the cinemas Saturday afternoon matinee. In the 70's practically every child in the Ferry attended this and it could get a bit chaotic. No speaking was allowed, and the Humphries would shush anyone who tried.

Although they were strict, I feel that the ladies may have been a bit slack with the cinema classifications. I was only five, yet I remember seeing some films that were definitely not "U" certificate.

The one that springs to mind involved a group of campers who were individually attacked and devoured by a large grizzly bear.

One scene, which I still recall, involved one camper being mercilessly battered between two trees by said grizzly!

To assist with keeping the matinee attendees in order, the sisters employed a young lad to act as usher. This lad once decided to bring along his girlfriend and the two of them started to canoodle in the back row. My sisters, cousins and I started to laugh and annoy them, and the lad kicked us out. My aunt was none too chuffed to have her afternoons peace destroyed by us trooping in. A telephone call was made to the Miss Humpries whereby my uncle used his influence as the cinema/family plumber and demanded justice for us. I am ashamed to say that the lad was dismissed, and our matinee trips restored…….

The Humphries sisters really do deserve a medal. The cinema housed 712 people so you can imagine how it must have been with that number of children. We were all under 14 and, while not bad kids, we could be a bit raucous – especially my boy cousins and their pals who sat at the back!

The Regal Saturday matinee was like a troupe of monkeys that were admirably managed by the ladies in black. They allowed us to go so far and would then reign us in if we overstepped the mark.

These sisters led us youngsters through all that the silver screen had to offer…. classics like Gone with the Wind (boring for children), to the bizarre Boy with the Green Hair (wouldn't get a second glance now) and also the scary blockbusters like Jaws.

They may not have owned or operated loads of cinemas like J B Milne, but these ladies were everything that going to the cinema represented. They ran a tight ship and, because of that, the Regal lives on in many a memory.

The Misses Humphries have long since departed this world, but I hope that by making them my leading ladies, I have gone some way into rewarding them for the hassle they suffered over many years of the children's Saturday matinee.

THE MAIN EVENT

(down Memory Lane)

I do remember seeing people with Jam jars for entry to the Rialto in Lochee. The Rialto and the Astoria were my locals as they were just shorts walks to get there. Forest Park was also walkable, and they had 'Chummy seats' i.e., Doubles with no central arm. I was a Harris pupil and often went to Grays cinema in Shepherds Loan. It had a corrugated iron roof and when raining the soundtrack couldn't be heard. Also, laddies would throw stones on it and as they fell down the noise was deafening. The Greens Playhouse was almost palatial with a huge foyer complete with café and of course the Divans. I used to attend the Gaumont on a Saturday morning as a schoolboy, still remember the song we sang at the beginning. First lines were "We come along on a Saturday morning greeting everybody with a smile". I hated the Kinnaird it had dreadful seats and was originally a meeting hall. The La Scala was dark and dingy. The best cinema in town was the Odeon at Coldside. Wonderful marble steps and brass handrails leading into a spacious auditorium. Happy days – Iain McM

Yes, being born in 1943 and then being a teenager in the 1950s, Dundee for me was a great place to live. Shopping, jobs and entertainment was plentiful. I think during this period there were around 25 cinemas in Dundee, so we were all spoilt for choice. I was particularly interested in war films which were mainly shown at the Playhouse or the Kinnaird and horror films (Hammer), which were mainly shown at the La Scala and several others. – Anon

My earliest memory of going to a cinema was to Grays. My mother took me there to see "Reach for the Sky" around 1955. Not exactly a kiddie's film! – Mike G

While in the Police I had to escort a group of local Councillors to the Tivoli to view a film to see if it was suitable for the Dundee viewing public. I'm not sure about the public but the Councillors certainly enjoyed it - DW

With regards to Grays cinema, in the summer when the projection room window above the entrance was open. I could hear the soundtrack's screams, gunshots, sirens in my bed across the road when at my grannies in the Dairy! Scary stuff for a wee laddie. Later she would never let me sit in 'the scratchers' (6d) seats, always at the back in the 1/3s. Then when I was older of course, 'the chummy seats'!! – Anon

I remember going to the Capitol to the Saturday morning children's matinees there. We would all queue up outside with our empty jam jars and a few pennies from mum & dad. This would be in the 50's. – Anon

Remember going to the ABC to see The Exorcist There was a priest outside, walking up and doon the queue, trying to persuade folk not to go in and clutching some holy water– Anon

Remember going to the Odeon and seeing Samson and Delilah, The Robe, Calamity Jane, Showboat and many others when I was primary school age. Laurel and Hardy films come to mind too. Probably cost 6d if you went at matinee times. Used to move to another seat to avoid being turned out at the end and watched the same film twice – Helen R

The song that we sang at the Gaumont club was "We come along on Saturday morning, greeting everybody with a smile. We come along on Saturday morning knowing that it's well worth while". As members of the GB club, we all intend to be good citizens when we grow up and champions of the free. – Ian G

In the late 1950s, in order to help pay for my motorbikes while on an apprentice's wages, I worked at the Reres Cinema in Broughty Ferry as a part-time projectionist. The projection room was equipped with two Kalee 8 carbon arc projectors which required constant attention in order to maintain the correct gap between the two carbon rods thus providing the best standard of white light for the film. I often remember standing with the projectionist with the projection room window open and looking out onto Gray Street during the Saturday afternoon matinee to watch the girls go by and forgetting about keeping the projector arcs set, only to hear shouting from one of the owners below to get it sorted (but in a bit more colourful language). When I watch antique collectable programmes on TV, I look back and regret not saving any of the film advertising posters which now fetch some astonishing prices at auction by collectors. – Bob T

There was a wee usherette in the Royalty, Baffin St, who used to help customers by flashing her torch at the chummy row and calling "Two together" – Bill F

My wife and were sitting in the chummy seats and found, instead of sharing one, we were occupying two, with the armrest between us. It amused us for some time – Conrad D.

We are speaking about the period from 1940 until approximately 1960. My picture house was the "Forest Park Cinema" sited at the corner of Forest Park Road and Forest Park Place and known locally as the "Forry". It was very fortunate that it missed being bombed by roughly 100 feet when a German bomber dropped his bombs on Dundee and instead took the frontage off the Power station opposite our tenement and removed all our windows. This was on the 5th of November 1940. The Germans, very decently, kept their visits till after the cinema was closed.
In general cinemas were often referred to as 'The showies'. The Forry was fairly basic with seats downstairs at 6d or 9d and upstairs 1/- or 1/6. They had chummy seats at the back which I was to discover later. I remember sitting downstairs, we weren't exactly rich, and thinking that the screen was a bit hazy with an awful lot of people smoking. One of the usherettes would come round with Walls ice cream during the performances and of course there was a rush to get there first with a lot of people having to stand up to let them past, it was the cheap seats after all and there wasn't much knee room. Speaking during the 'fulm' was not allowed and the usherettes would quickly light up the speakers with their torch and threaten them with 'ye'll be thrown oot'. On one occasion, when I was about ten, I pleaded with my mother to let me go and see 'The Case of the Scarlet Claw' and she warned me that it was supposed to be very scary but as my pal, Chicky Broon was going, she let me. Well, she was right, it was scary, and we ran all the way home. Later that night before I went to bed, I pleaded with my mother to let me pee in the kitchen sink as our toilet was outside and it would be pitch dark, just the type of night for the man with the scarlet claw!

Although the Forry was our regular cinema being just across the road, we also went to Gray's cinema in Shepherds Loan, the State in Bellfield Street, and the Princess in the Hawkhill. We rarely went to the city cinemas and although I tried the kids' club in the Gaumont on Saturday mornings I didn't like it as at that time I was quite reticent and found the noise from the general babble and shouting was too much for me and that was from the young patrons! When Hopalong Cassidy was shown there were cheers and boos for the baddies when they appeared. I do remember thinking that for all the fights Hopalong was in his hat remained firmly on his head. Roy Rogers was shown as well as a very early Flash Gordon. - AS

My aunty Mary who stayed in Lochee used to go to the town cinemas two or three times a week in the afternoons as my uncle worked at nights with the Dundee Corporation. And there was a good choice in the centre with the Gaumont, La Scala, Kinnaird, and the Greens Playhouse but as soon as they bought a TV she stopped going as did a lot of people. – Alfie S

I used to go to the Gaumont, and it was 3d in the stalls; 6d in the balcony. Kids in the balcony used to shower the stalls with lolly sticks etc. Usually there would be a feature film plus an episode from an American cowboy series e.g., The Lone Ranger, The Cisco Kid etc. Feature films had to be fairly short to fit into the morning session. The only one I can recall is The Boy with Green Hair. Occasionally there would be a live performance: a 'yoyo' demonstration, or, famously, Roy Rogers with his horse, Trigger. As far as I remember, the only advantage of club membership was having your birthday announced. An embarrassment which I was careful to avoid- Bill F

In the late 1950s / early 1960s, I had a girlfriend at the time whose aunt was a supervisor at the Playhouse, and we used to get free tickets to use upstairs for the notorious Golden Divans. Yes, a lot of "nonsense" went on up there I can assure you. – Bob T

I went to the Astoria, sometimes 3 times a week, loved how you just go in and watch the film half way through and wait and watch for a second time, changed the film over on a Thursday, would get 4 pineapple chunks for a 1d, 4 black jacks for a 1d, M & B bar 2d, and a bag of chips sometime fritters for 6d coming home. Happy days – May Mac

I remember when I was at school, we were sent to the Tivoli to watch a Health Education Film and me and my pals joked (and secretly hoped) that they would show the wrong film. They were known for some saucy films – Frank M

Me and my best mate and our then boyfriends got chucked out of the Galleon pub. We were 16 and headed despondently to the Vic on Victoria Road. "Enter the Dragon" was what the billboard said. Must have been1973 or '74. Great let's go in. So, there was a fella singing and nobody looked remotely Far Eastern. We were all very confused. The lady in front kept turning round and asking us to shut up as she and her grandkids couldn't hear. Eh. What the heck's going on? Basically, chucked out the pub and then paid to get in to watch the Student Prince. They used to change the billboards the night before…Oh the ignominy. Still laugh about it yet. Great times. – Fiona B

I remember going to the Gaumont on a Saturday morning in the early 60's as a 10 year old. I lived just off Victoria Road so was close to the cinema. Most of the children in the road where I lived went too so we all went together and often filled a whole row in the cinema. We would visit sweet shop on the way. It cost 3d for stalls and 6d for balcony. There would be some entertainment and a sing song before we would see a cartoon then the main film. My favourite film being Zorro. One of the songs we used to sing was " We come along on Saturday morning greeting everybody with a smile, we come along on Saturday morning making life worthwhile. If I remember correctly, we were there from 9am until 12 noon. Lovely memories. – Elizabeth S

I was born in 1942 so was probably going to the cinema in the fifties. I grew up in Bellefield Avenue, so it was only a short walk along the Magdalen Green and up Shepherd's Loan to the cinema (Grays) which was near the top of the road. It was very cheap to get in and you went in usually in the middle of a film and sat through the whole programme. There was the main film, a B film and the Pathe News. In the days before TV it was the first visual news we saw. Sadly, it was always very smoky. I don't remember what we paid but it was very little. – Pat U

I was born and brought up for my first 15 years in the West end of Dundee where we had our own group of cinemas. Gray's cinema in Shepherds Loan, Princess on the Hawkhill, State in Bellfield Street (now Whitehall theatre), Forest Park in Forest Park Place, Regal cinema Smalls Wynd, Cinerama Tay St. Spoiled for choice!!!

In 50's and 60's there were 2 films per evening, an A and a B film. The B film tended to be a Western. My favourite!! Also, we went into town to the bigger cinemas. Tarzan films at the Kinnaird in Bank Street. (With "chummy seats in the balcony.) Best memory was seeing, in awe! Space Odyssey 2001 by Stanley Kubrick on huge CinemaScope wide screen cinema at the ABC in the Seagate. Finally " going along on a Saturday morning" to the Kids King's Club at the Kings (Gaumont) cinema in the Wellgate (opposite the Wellgate Centre) to see Flash Gordon Getting older the Golden Divans at the Greens Playhouse was the favourite. Also the Odeon in Strathmartine Rd for Disney's Fantasia. A point to note, was the King's and the Playhouse doubled up as theatres. We saw Billy Fury and Joe Brown at the Kings. Adam Faith and the Batchelors at the Playhouse. Absolutely great memories. - George Mc

I remember visiting Greens Playhouse many times, however one occasion really sticks out in my mind. A lady friend and I visited the cinema and went to the Golden Divans, or Dive-ins as we used to call them. These were reclining beds where people would take someone special. They also had the added bonus of having curtains you could close for privacy. On this occasion myself and my friend closed the curtains and eventually fell asleep. We woke up to a darkness and a closed cinema. We did not fancy staying the night and having to explain ourselves to everyone, so we made our escape through the fire exit. This triggered the alarm and we both legged it as fast as we could up Tay Street. – Anon

I was at the Forry and the picture, as they were called at the time, not movie as we are subject to Americanisms now, and it was a cowboy film. There was a wee laddie sitting in front of me who was really engrossed, and you could tell, as he was on the edge of his seat during a confrontation between him and a group of baddies. As luck would have it the hero ran out of ammunition, and as he tried to fire again the hammer came down on an empty chamber and the wee lad shouted 'He's run out o' ceps' and he turned to his Mum, but she just shook her head. To explain - 'Ceps' or Caps were small rolls of paper approximately 3/8 inch across with small dots spaced along the length which were filled with an amount of powder which when hit with a small hammer would ignite and create a small bang. This was exactly what was required in a small boy's armoury in fighting these darn Injuns and these persistent baddies. The juvenile six guns had a small cylindrical chamber where the caps went and if you threaded one end through the entry to the feeding device and then to the hammer you were 'a' the road 'to fight again. These Caps came in a roll and were sold in a round cardboard container at all supply depots in the city i.e. Paper shops. – Alfie S

Every Saturday afternoon me, my two sisters and our 3 girl cousins were sent to the Regal in the Ferry. We saw many films there, including Jaws and I remember that everyone in the cinema screamed at the scary bits (like the head rolling out of the boat). If that week's film hadn't arrived, they had back up – Lost in the Desert which was a very depressing film about a wee lad and his dog that were marooned in the desert after a plane crash.. That film must have been shown at least three times every year – PM

I used to go to the Victoria (Vicky) or fleapit as we later called it and have to say it was pretty low down in the order of cinemas to visit. On one visit I came home with a few guests and had to use special shampoo and a nit comb. On another occasion I was sitting when, during a film, a large chunk of plaster fell from the ceiling – that was the last time I visited. It wasn't too long after that it was condemned – Anon

When I was wee, my mum thought it would be a good idea to take me to see Bambi at the Vic. I must have been about 6 and remember that I cried to much when Bambi's mum was shot that I had to be taken out of the cinema……I have never watched that film again! – AW

My Dad used to tell me that when he was young, he and his friends would scour the local neighbourhood for empty bottles and jam jars. None of them were well off, but they could get entry into the cinema for two jam jars or bottles. The idea was that if they presented clean jars, they would get admission. One time my dad was a bit over enthusiastic and took in a jar with some jam scrapings still in it; the cinema took it, but he got into trouble by the ticket attendant and my granny. – Anon

When the Star Trek films first came out, I went to see it at the then ABC cinema in the Seagate. I wasn't a huge "Trekkie" so just went in normal clothes. I felt a bit out numbered because practically everyone else was there in full Star Trek uniforms, complete with Spock ears. – E. McD

CLOSING CREDITS

KEY (GET A) GRIP – Maura Bowman (Matheson)

LAPTOP SUPPLIER – Dad (W D E Wares)

CATERING – Frank Mulgrew

BEST BOY (always) – Austin Lindsay

DRAMATIC ARTISTRY – Cecelia Lindsay

CATERING (WINE) – Annie Nicol

GENERAL SUPPORT – Colette Robbie, Gabby Mulgrew

GUEST ARTIST - REX THE DOG

No animals suffered during the writing of this book; the guinea pigs (Lola and Trixie) were fed and cleaned, and the dogs (Daisy and Gem) received regular walks and snacks.

Printed in Great Britain
by Amazon